Are You Radio Prepared?

Brad Smith

Are You Radio Prepared?

How to Always Be Able to Communicate in Any Emergency Situation

By Brad Smith

Copyright 2012

Published by Brad's Tech Publishing

brad73@radioprepared.com

www.radioprepared.com

Disclaimer

The information given in this book is solely for educational and entertainment purposes and in no way should be construed to be legal, medical or professional advice. The author and publisher assume no liability for any actions taken by any individual or group that is considered illegal, based on information in this book.

CONTENTS

ACKNOWLEDGMENTS

I would like to thank my book consultant, Joan Rhine, for her expertise in all areas of book publishing.

Thanks to all my writing club friends, the Tulsa NightWriters, for their encouragement.

And, especially, thanks to my family for all their support.

Introduction

Does your family have an emergency plan to ride out the aftermath of a disaster? Can you imagine anything more frightening than not being able to communicate with loved ones, to know that they are all right and to report you are as well?

The Red Cross and FEMA websites have online checklists to follow in the event of an emergency, but they leave out critical information. They tell you to have an emergency radio with AM, FM and Weather capabilities but don't explain how to find the stations that are provided with emergency information. They don't explain why cell phones may not operate during a disaster. They don't tell you how you can stay in touch with family and friends by radio.

In the Event of an Emergency

This book explains how to actually use those emergency radios in plain language, and in a step-by-step format.

- In plain language you will learn about different radios that are available to you and how to use. With a little training, on your own and with this book, you can use two-way radios to communicate with your loved ones, regardless of whether phone and cell towers are functioning. In addition, you can use these same radios to stay abreast of changing conditions and changing emergency situations.

- Should you need to talk farther than about 25 miles, amateur (ham) radio is an option that is easier to obtain than in any time in history. This book explains how to listen to hams in your area or world-wide. If you decide you want to get a license to transmit, Chapter 5 is an introduction to ham radio with steps for passing the entry-level Technician license. No Morse Code test is necessary for this nor the two higher-level licenses.

- In the unlikely event of a very large, long-term disaster, a community FM radio station can be put on the air to help disseminate important news for the immediate area. Step-by-step instructions in this book explain how to set up and run a micro FM station and what equipment is needed.

- Because we're used to searching online for all preparedness information, it is wise to keep a copy of important web pages. Create a folder on your computer to hold the web sites. Go to the page you would like to keep and select File/Save As, or File/Save Page As, and specify "Web Page, Complete." Select your folder and Save. When the Internet is down you can still access these important pages on your computer. Just start your browser and select File/Open and browse to the saved page.

Practice! Don't buy radio equipment and store it away with your food. Learn to operate your radios and practice monthly. Don't wait for an emergency to happen and waste time looking for batteries or a radio manual. Have a plan and post it where your whole family can see it.

CHAPTER 1
LOCAL NEWS AND INFORMATION

One of the items included in most emergency lists is a portable radio. Where will you be when the lights go out? How will you know what is going on outside your dark and lonely home? Find your flashlight, then your emergency radio and batteries. Local news is the most important thing you'll need to keep up with in an emergency. A portable AM/FM radio is essential whether you stay home or travel to an alternate safe location. Have plenty of spare batteries available. A radio that includes weather band will let you hear local weather and other government announcements. Amber alerts are now broadcast on weather radio. If the emergency covers a wide area, other messages may be added to the weather radio broadcasts.

In addition to batteries, some emergency radios have hand cranks. These radios have rechargeable batteries built in. The hand crank is a dynamo charger that will recharge these built-in batteries. You must crank for several minutes in order to listen to the radio. Keeping the volume low or using a headset or ear buds will make the batteries last longer.

One example of a good emergency radio is the Eton FR360. This radio has been endorsed by the American Red Cross. Some models of this radio have the Red Cross emblem on them. The radio can be powered by internal rechargeable batteries, regular batteries, or by a wall charger (not included). Charging of the internal rechargeable batteries can be accomplished by cranking, solar power or with the wall charger. Recharging by solar power takes a long time, and the radio must be in direct sunlight. If your cell phone can be recharged by a USB cable, you can use this radio to recharge it. You must use the hand crank, solar cell or wall charger to charge your cell phone.

A sister radio to the Eton FR360 mentioned above is the Eton FR600. The FR600 has county selectable weather radio alerts ("SAME" system).It includes shortwave (SW) but does not have single sideband (SSB) capabilities for hams. It will pick up international broadcast stations. The tuning is done by buttons and is somewhat difficult but it does receive well. Don't buy the FR600 for shortwave, buy it for the SAME alert system. See later chapters for shortwave information.

Weather

There are seven weather channels. Listen to each channel to determine which one is in use in your area. For best reception extend the antenna located on the back of the radio. The antenna should be oriented vertically for best reception. The FR360 has an alert function that will turn on the radio when there is a weather alert. You cannot select alerts by county with this radio. There is also an alarm clock built in as well as an LED flashlight.

In the event of your local weather station being off the air, you can still receive stations from other cities.

Step by step

- Turn on the radio by pressing the button for the type of power you want to use.

- Extend the telescoping antenna.

- Adjust the volume to a low level to reduce white noise that is characteristic of these frequencies.

- Set the channel selector to each Weather channel (marked WB1 –WB7 on the FR360) until you hear a station.

- If more than one station is heard, listen until you can determine that you have the right station for your area. Make a note of your local channel.

- You may turn on the alert function by pressing the Alert button while the radio is on and the volume is at a level that will get your attention.

The steps for your radio may be different. Refer to your owner's manual.

The SAME county alert system

SAME means Specific Area Message Encoding. This system allows you to specify alerts by counties. You may set this for more than one county so that you get alerts for the region.

Here's how to set up SAME alerting on the FR600. Your radio will be somewhat different but you should have no problem. Have your manual ready for reference.

Step by step

- First, find the SAME codes for the counties that you would like to include. This web site lists all the SAME codes: http://www.nws.noaa.gov/nwr/indexnw.htm#sametable Click on your state, then write down the codes for the counties you selected.

- Turn the big selector knob on the right-hand side of the radio to "OFF."

- Press the MENU button at the upper right of the display.

- Press the up and down arrows buttons at the right of the display until you see "WEATHER" in the display.

- Press SELECT at the upper left of the display. The SELECT button is also marked "RBDS."

- Press the up and down buttons until your local weather channel shows at the right side of the display.

- Press SELECT to save this.

- Press MENU, then up and down buttons until you see "ALERT MODE" in the display.

- Press SELECT again, then up and down buttons to select the alert mode you want.

- Press SELECT to save this.

- Press MENU, then up and down buttons until you see "COUNTY CODE" in the display.

- Press SELECT, then up and down buttons to select MULTI if you are setting more than one county, SINGL for one county, or ALL to alert for all counties served by this station.

- Press SELECT again. If you are entering one county, press SELECT to skip over the "01" to set the country code. If entering multiple counties, use the up and down buttons to select county 01, 02, 03 etc. Press SELECT to move to the county code.

- The county code is six digits. The first digit space will be blinking. Press the up and down buttons to enter the first digit. Press the "right arrow" button (left side of display) to proceed to the next digit.

- If in MULTI mode, press SELECT to enter the next code. Press the down button to go to the next code entry. Press SELECT again to enter the next 6-digit code.

- When all finished, press SELECT then MENU to exit.

This may sound complicated, but once you actually do each step with the radio at hand, it's not hard.

FM

Most radio listening is on the FM band where static is rare and there are many music stations to choose from. Some of your favorite stations may be programmed by a computer playlist or a satellite feed. You may not be able to get timely information from these in an emergency. News / Talk stations are beginning to appear on FM nowadays. These will carry local, state and national emergency news. What if you don't have a good news FM station or if your station is off the air for some reason?

If a nearby town is less affected by the disaster than your town, you can listen to their stations. You may be able to receive FM stations from as far away as 100 miles any time of year. Extending the telescoping antenna on your radio will give the best reception of distant FM stations. Using your radio with the antenna at higher locations is better – upstairs, on a hill, etc. Local weather will affect FM reception. Overcast conditions, especially in early or late summer, can cause reception of stations even farther away but not as reliably as local or nearby stations. FM reception is generally the same 24 hours a day.

You may be familiar with the frequency range of the FM band, 88 to 108 megahertz (MHz). There are 100 frequencies, or channels, in the U.S. FM band. Stations are assigned in odd-numbered steps, e.g., 98.1, 98.3, 98.5, 98.7. Some stations may identify as having an even number after the decimal point, like 98.6, but this is just for show.

Step by step

- If you know the frequencies of nearby stations, tune to them with a tuning knob or enter the frequencies directly via a keypad.

- To tune for stations, first: do not use the SEEK or SCAN buttons. These features may skip over a station because the signal is not very strong.

- If your radio has a round tuning knob, start at one end of the band and slowly tune.

- If your radio has a keypad with up and down buttons or "TUNE" buttons, start at one end of the band and press the buttons until a station comes in.

- Write down the frequency of any station you would like to listen to later.

- If the station you want to hear is very weak, you can go to higher ground. If that is not possible, try a random length of any kind of wire thrown up on the roof or into a tree. Connect the wire to the telescoping antenna by removing some of the insulation from the wire and wrapping it around the antenna or use an alligator clip or a binder clip to hold the wire tight to the antenna.

- Tip: using a headset or ear buds can greatly extend battery life.

AM

While FM stations have better sound and less static than AM stations, AM can cover longer distances. If you can't get an FM station that provides disaster news and information, try AM. There are many News / Talk stations on AM. Also, at night your AM radio can pick up stations from long distances.

During the daytime, AM reception should be about the same as FM. The antenna on the radio will not help AM reception. The AM antenna is inside the radio. You may improve reception of an AM station by rotating the radio slightly. This can help in two ways. Rotating the radio until the station you are listening to is loudest is usually what you would do. However, if there is another station interfering with the one you want to hear, you can rotate the radio until the reception of the interfering station is lowest, allowing you to hear your station better.

Nighttime is a whole different story with AM. Starting at dusk and continuing until sunrise, you will pick up stations from hundreds or even thousands of miles away. If you are only interested in local stations, there could be a problem with interference. If you are interested in hearing what is happening in other areas, this can be ideal. There are high-powered radio stations in most states that you can pick up. Weather conditions will affect what you hear.

Another thing to note about AM radio is that there is much more interference and noise than on FM. Static and crashes are caused by lightning storms all over the earth. If these are stronger than the station you are listening to, it can be hard to listen. Rotating the radio will help to some extent but you may have to switch to an FM station if it is unacceptable. One possible good thing about static is that you can tell the weather by how often and how strong the static crashes are. As the static gets louder and closer together, you know there is an approaching storm.

A "whining" sound is caused by two AM stations on the same frequency. Rotating the radio may help but you may just have to wait a period of time until one of the stations becomes strong enough to overcome the other.

The U.S. AM band covers the frequencies from 540 kilohertz (kHz) to 1,700 kHz. You also may be able to hear traffic information stations on 530 and 1,710 kHz. These stations only cover a few miles. Generally the comma is not used for frequencies from 1,000 kHz up. So, 1,170 kHz is usually shown as 1170. Stations are assigned frequencies every 10 kHz, e.g., 850, 860, 870, 880. If you happen to live in an area where you can hear European stations, such as the east coast, you will need a radio that can tune every 9 kHz.

Step by step

- If you have frequencies for AM stations in other cities, you may use a keypad to directly enter them. Remember to rotate the radio before you give up on a station.

- To search for stations, as with FM, do not use the SCAN or SEEK buttons.

- Start at one end of the band and tune up or down with your tuning knob or up and down TUNE buttons.

- Use of a headset or ear buds will not only save battery power but also keep from annoying other people with the often loud static on AM.

Scanners

If you want to go beyond what AM and FM stations are telling you and listen behind the scenes, a scanner radio can be used to receive police, fire, government officials, etc. The problem with scanners is that they are hard to program and you have to learn all about frequencies, trunking and all sorts of other technical info. But there is one scanner that is made for the rest of us.

The Uniden HomePatrol scanner is the easiest scanner to use. To set up this scanner, you type in your zip code and that's it. The scanner then programs itself with all your local radio systems. Search for it online. It's pricey but is as easy to use as your AM/FM radio. If you travel to another area, just enter the new zip code.

Ham radio operators can be heard on scanners. There are networks of hams who volunteer during emergencies and they use Very High Frequency (VHF) and Ultra High Frequency (UHF) bands for local communication. More on that later.

Handheld Radio Receivers

There are several types of handheld radios. Research these before you buy. If all you need is a scanner you have a big selection of handheld scanners. Some of them will receive trunking systems like police and fire. Check with your local Radio Shack store or, better yet, find a ham radio operator near you. Hams are very helpful with all kinds of radios, not just ham radios. Plus, you will have someone to work with if you want to get a ham license. To find a ham near you, go to

http://wireless2.fcc.gov/UlsApp/UlsSearch/searchAmateur.jsp and you can get a list of hams in your zip code or city. Just knock on their door!

There are handhelds that are not primarily scanners but receive VHF and UHF frequencies. A couple of brands are ICOM and AOR. These provide a wider range of frequencies than you may ever need but are great radios. Most of these will have analog cell phone frequencies blocked. Some even cover SW as well. We'll get into two-way handhelds later.

A word about batteries

If you have rechargeable batteries in your radio, be sure to use the radio each month and then recharge the batteries. Can your radio be operated with conventional non-rechargeable batteries in case your rechargeable batteries die? If the electricity is out you may not be able to recharge. Keep a good supply of batteries on hand. The shelf life of batteries is about eight years and you do not need to keep them in a refrigerator.

Summary

- A portable radio is essential for emergencies.

- Weather band is important. County-selectable alert (SAME) is better.

- FM is good for local stations and some neighboring towns.

- AM is good for local News / Talk in the daytime and longer distance stations at night.

- A scanner will let you hear local police, fire, hams, etc. first hand.

- Some handheld receivers are higher quality than portables.

- Keep and rotate a supply of batteries.

CHAPTER 2
WORLD-WIDE NEWS AND INFORMATION

Shortwave Radio

Many preparedness guides include having a radio that will receive shortwave broadcast (SWBC) stations. The traditional reason to have a shortwave capable radio is to receive a world view of news. This was true for many years and may still be useful today but many foreign governments are cutting off funding for their international shortwave (SW) services. There are stations going off the air every month. They are now "broadcasting" via Internet audio streaming. If your Internet connection is broken, of course, you won't be able to listen on your computer or mobile device. I offer you a better reason for having a shortwave radio later in the chapter.

What is shortwave, exactly?

Think about an AM radio with a "slide rule" dial, similar to a number line, showing 540 to 1700. Imagine that you can tune all the way to the right (1700) and keep going. The frequencies above 1700 and all the way up to 30,000 kilohertz (kHz), or 30 megahertz (MHz) are shortwave. Shortwave is sometimes referred to as HF (high frequency). There are sections, or bands, of shortwave frequencies that are assigned to many services. There are ships, planes, ham operators and broadcast stations to name a few. Shortwave broadcast stations use AM and are susceptible to static and fading.

Reception on SW is similar to traditional AM. There are some major differences, too. Some SW frequencies work better at night, typically below 10 MHz. Above 10 MHz is better for daytime reception. Weather is always a factor, storms causing the worst conditions for reception. A major player in SW is the sunspot cycle. Sunspots decrease and increase on an average cycle of eleven years. When sunspots are low, SW reception is lousy but usable. When sunspots are high, SW works very well. The next maximum at this writing could be in 2013 or 2014.

Shortwave Broadcast Listening

Shortwave listening is popular worldwide. That fact is why U.S. SW stations are generally meant to broadcast to other countries, but can still be heard here. More Americans listen to the thousands of traditional AM and FM stations and Internet stations than SWBC stations. While SW listening can result in static and fading at times, there are a few SWBC stations in the U.S. that can be heard clearly, for example: Voice of America, Radio Marti and several commercial SW broadcasters.

If the emergency is nation-wide and local stations are off the air or you just want to get some news from far away then you can listen to SWBC stations. Some better-known foreign stations are the BBC (UK), Radio Moscow (Russia) and HCJB (Ecuador). Due to the nature of SW, many of the larger stations broadcast on several different frequencies based on time of day and the area of the world they are targeting.

Tuning In Shortwave Broadcast Stations

Tuning shortwave broadcast stations is similar to tuning AM stations. The key to finding stations is knowing the bands and frequencies to tune and when to tune them. You can also just tune through the band to see what you can hear. There are magazines and websites that list SWBC stations and good times to try to listen.

Shortwave bands are identified by the approximate wavelength of the band given in meters. For example, one SWBC band is 49 meters. Each band has a frequency range that you can tune. For 49 meters, the range is 5900 kHz to 6200 kHz. Your radio may show frequencies in kHz (same as kilocycles or kc on older radios) or in MHz (megacycles – mc on older radios). If your radio shows frequencies in MHz then the 49 meter band ranges from 5.900 to 6.200 MHz. Think of the "meter band" as just a name for a band of frequencies.

SWBC stations are usually spaced every 5 or 10 kHz, for example, 6000, 6005, 6010, 6015 etc. Most stations transmit in AM mode. Occasionally you will run across a station that is transmitting in single sideband. This could be upper sideband (USB) or lower sideband (LSB). When this occurs you hear a "Donald Duck" sounding voice or strange sounding music. Set your mode switch to SSB, USB, LSB or CW and tune slowly up and down to clarify the signal. Single sideband is essential for listening to hams on shortwave.

Since fewer and fewer stations broadcast on shortwave, in a large disaster some new (or old) ones may show up. Be aware that many SWBC stations are heavy into propaganda so listen with discretion.

A word about time

Due to the world-wide locations of shortwave stations, local time is not announced. Shortwave stations use Universal Coordinated Time (UTC). UTC is also known as Greenwich Mean Time (GMT) and Zulu time. UTC starts at the zero degrees longitude (prime) meridian that passes through Greenwich, UK. Time will be given in military style, 1900 for 7:00 PM, etc.

To convert UTC to your local time:
Eastern Standard Time, subtract 5 hours.
Central Standard Time, subtract 6 hours.
Mountain Standard Time, subtract 7 hours.
Pacific Standard Time, subtract 8 hours.

Eastern Daylight Saving Time, subtract 4 hours.
Central Daylight Saving Time, subtract 5 hours.
Mountain Daylight Saving Time, subtract 6 hours.
Pacific Daylight Saving Time, subtract 7 hours.

To convert your local time to UTC, just ADD the number of hours.

SWBC Bands

120 meters, 2300 – 2495 kHz
90 meters, 3200 – 3400 kHz
75 meters, 3900 – 4000 kHz
60 meters, 4750 - 5060 kHz
49 meters, 5900 – 6200 kHz
41 meters, 7200 – 7450 kHz
31 meters, 9400 – 9900 kHz
25 meters, 11,600 – 12,100 kHz
22 meters, 13,570 – 13,870 kHz
19 meters, 15,100 – 15,800 kHz

16 meters, 17,480 – 17,900 kHz
15 meters, 18,900 – 19,020 kHz
13 meters, 21,450 – 21,850 kHz
11 meters, 25,600 – 26,100 kHz

Here's a general description of the bands.

120 m – a "tropical" band (in or near the tropics), not heard well in the US.
90 m – tropical band
75 m – shared with ham radio 80 meter band, noisy, good at night but may have a lot of interference from ham operators.
60 m – tropical band but some US SWBC stations are in this range. Nights are best reception.
49 m – popular band, daytime ok, nighttime better.
41 m – Shared with 40 meter ham band. Good in daytime, better at night.
31 m – most popular SWBC band. Day or night.
25 m – Daytime better.
22 m – Daytime better.
19 m – Daytime. May not hear any stations at night.
16 m – Same as 19m.
15 m – Same, not used much.
13 m – Day only, may be useful only when sunspot cycle is at peak.
11 m – Same as 13m.

Not all radios will have all bands. Some radios can be set to the exact frequency of a station, if you know it, by keying it in from a keypad. Or you can key in the lowest frequency for a particular band then tune upwards from there.

Step by step

- Set your radio's mode to AM.

- If your radio has a "band switch", select one of the shortwave bands.

- Set the volume to a level that is comfortable considering the noise and static.

- Headphones / ear buds are suggested.

- If your radio has a keypad, enter the starting frequency for one of the shortwave bands.

- Slowly tune upwards in frequency. If you have a button that increases the frequency by 5 kHz, you can use it to tune.

- When you hear a station tune up or down slightly to clarify it.

- If the station fades out, just wait a few seconds and it may fade back in.

- Write down the frequency for any stations that you would like to listen to in the future.

- Listen to the station identification, normally at the top of the hour and sometimes more often. Alternate times and frequencies may be given.

The Better Reason to Have Shortwave

Amateur radio operators (hams) can also be found in their own bands on SW. Hams handle emergency communications on a regular basis and you can tune them in. Even if a disaster is limited to a small area, such as a tornado or earthquake, you may be able to hear them at your location. Hams' first priority is life and death communication. They call this "priority traffic." When priority traffic is not needed, they handle messages concerning loved ones getting in touch. This is called "health and welfare" traffic. Any less important messages are called "routine traffic."

Hams generally do not use AM transmission. They use single sideband (SSB). To listen to hams, your radio must have one or more of these designations or features: SSB, LSB, USB (not a computer connector), CW, BFO. When you buy a shortwave radio, be sure that it receives SSB and includes the amateur bands. A radio with "general coverage" usually means it will receive from 3 to 30 MHz inclusive. All but one SW ham band is included in this range. Turn on one of these modes before tuning in the ham bands. There is a list of several of the frequency bands for hams in Chapter Five.

An outside antenna, usually just a wire strung out as high and far as possible, is best for picking up hams. If your radio has a connection for a SW antenna, use that. If not, wire an alligator clip to the end of the wire (remove the plastic insulation) and clip it to the telescoping antenna on your radio. If you don't have an alligator clip or perhaps a binder clip, just wrap the exposed wire tightly around the antenna. When tuning SSB, you must tune very slowly until you get to the clearest point.

In an emergency, the hams will usually have organized

communications controlled by one operator. This is called a "net", short for network. The emergency net is called a directed net. In this kind of net the control operator (net control), directs when each station speaks. This minimizes confusion. The best band for daytime listening is the 20-meter band. The frequency range for SSB in the 20-meter band is 14.140 MHz to 14.350 MHz, USB. Two regular nets that you may hear are:

14.300 USB – **Maritime Mobile Service Net**, assisting boats and ships.

14.325 USB – **National Hurricane Center.**
If the NHC is not heard on 14.325 in the evening or nighttime, you may be able to hear it on 7.268 MHz LSB or 3.950 MHz LSB.

Emergency nets may appear on any frequency in these bands so tune around. For your state-wide net information, find the Amateur Radio Emergency Service (ARES) website for your state. The different nets will be listed.

Tuning hams is similar to tuning SWBC stations, as above, just tune more slowly. Single sideband can be tricky to tune. When you hear a high-pitched tone, tune down in pitch until the voice is clear. This could mean tuning up or down in frequency.

Summary

- A radio that has the capability to receive SWBC stations will let you listen to world-wide news.

- Some SWBC stations transmit propaganda for a certain country or cause.

- A radio that includes singe sideband modes and the correct frequency coverage will let you listen to ham stations.

CHAPTER 3
TWO-WAY COMMUNICATION (LICENSE-FREE)

When the twin towers fell, an amazing thing happened. People began calling their loved ones and asking, "Are you okay?" It didn't matter that some of them were a thousand miles from New York. They called anyway. In any kind of disaster this is the primary concern. Most of us were fortunate to be able to use cell, office and home phones. The people near ground zero were not. The cell systems were overloaded or inoperable.

Wire line telephone

Your first line of communication, literally, is a home telephone line. Many have given this up, choosing to use only their cell phone or VoIP phones through an Internet connection. If your Internet stops, you have no phone service. OK, so you use your cell phone instead. What if cell service is down or overloaded?

The plain old telephone service (POTS) is the most reliable network we have. Unless your central telephone office is blown away, you should have reliable phone service. Also needed is a plain, cheap phone that does not require AC power. If power goes out, you can still make calls with the old-fashioned, non-cordless phones. They are powered by the phone company. Your local phone company has backup batteries and generators that will allow phone service to operate many days without the electric company.

If you need to make a long distance (LD) call and your long distance provider is out of commission, there are short codes that you can dial that will connect you to different long distance providers. For example, if your LD provider is Sprint and they are not working, you can dial 10288 + the number to use AT&T service.

Why cell phones won't work in a disaster

Cell phone plans are like fitness center plans. They are oversold because the providers know that not everyone will be using the service at the same time. When a disaster happens, the cell phone lines can be busy for long periods of time. If towers are blown down or destroyed, it could be days or weeks. Sometimes text messages will get through when voice traffic is too busy. If the infrastructure is damaged, text messaging won't work.

I live in Oklahoma. I had a conversation with a California resident. He wondered how we lived with the threat of tornadoes. I said, "You can hide from a tornado but you can't hide from an earthquake." We never had earthquakes in Oklahoma – until 2011. It was mild but shook the house. We decided to call our kids to see if they felt it. We could not get a cell call through for 15 minutes! What would happen in a true emergency?

Radio Communication with Family & Friends

Radio waves are not susceptible to being shut down by disasters, the government or anything. Radio waves travel freely through the air and many solid objects. There are many types of two-way radios available. What systems are best for your situation? Any communication is better than none but planning ahead with the best radios for your situation will enhance your communication when the time comes.

You may think that using the latest and greatest high tech radios you can find would be best. Not necessarily. More sophisticated radio systems such as police, fire, etc. depend on computers and relay stations. These radios are hard to come by and if you do use them, you could be tracked and relieved of the equipment, maybe even arrested. Keep it simple so that everyone in your family can operate the radios with ease.

Amateur (ham) radio is the best choice for radio communication. The good news is that hams have privileges on many different frequencies. Some are good for local communication and some for long distances (DX). The bad news is that each person who uses ham radio must have their own individual license. The other good news is that it is much easier to pass the license exams than in the past. The requirement for a Morse Code test has been removed.

But what if your family does not want to become hams? My three daughters grew up with radios in the house but I could never get them interested. There are license-free radio services that can be used by the general public. Over all, ham radio is better but these other services are good for local and city-wide communication. Designate one person in your family to get a ham license and be the gateway to organized emergency organizations.

Citizen's Radio Services

The Federal Communications Commission (FCC) has set aside certain frequencies for use by the general public. No license is necessary for these services, except for GMRS, see below. They are licensed "by rule" which means you must follow the FCC rules or you may be fined or even imprisoned.

CB (Citizen's Band)

CB has been around for many years. Radios are not expensive. The range for CB can be up to a mile or two between cars or over 10 miles between houses if outside antennas are used. CB is not used much outside of truckers and travelers and could be a good choice for local talking. Just listening to channel 19 while on the road can get you good information on weather and traffic. The downside to CB is that it uses high frequencies (HF), also known as shortwave. Signals on CB can travel across the U.S. and even to some foreign countries. The sunspot cycle affects this phenomenon. Sunspots increase and decrease on an approximate 11 year cycle. The more sunspots, the more the signals "skip" from the ionosphere back to earth at a distance. When sunspot numbers are high, CB becomes almost useless for local communication and this could last up to three years. The next sunspot peak could be in 2013 or in 2014.

FRS (Family Radio Service)

These are the handheld radios you see for sale in many stores. FRS operates on UHF frequencies which are local in nature. They have transmitting power of ½ watt (500 milliwatts). These radios are great for traveling in a caravan, hiking, going to the mall, etc. Don't believe the range claims on the packages. You will not be able to talk 20 or 30 miles with these unless you and the person you are talking to are on high hills on either side of a lake. The main problem is the height of the antenna. Antennas on FRS radios are not removable. The only way you can get better reception is to move to higher ground. Figure on about a mile if both people are standing on the ground with not too many buildings or vegetation in between.

If you have a two-story house, go upstairs. If at the mall, climb the stairs to a higher level. UHF radio range depends on "line of sight." If you can see the other person, you can talk to them. Line of sight extends past the visible horizon. This is called the radio horizon. Radio waves will follow the curvature of the earth for a short distance.

FRS is assigned 14 channels. Seven of these are shared with GMRS (see below). Seven are FRS only. The other channels you see on most radios (15 through 22) are GMRS channels. GMRS is a licensed service but the general public does not know this. It is against the law to transmit on these channels without a license, but it is impossible to enforce. The Federal Communications Commission (FCC) is considering removing the licensing requirement for GMRS.

I don't recommend using "privacy" codes. Turn this OFF. Turn off any "call tones" and "roger beeps."

GMRS (General Mobile Radio Service)

GMRS is a UHF radio service. At present you must have a license for this service. The license costs $80 for 10 years. It covers your entire family, cousins, in-laws or anybody you say is family. GMRS can use higher power radios and mobile or home (base) antennas to increase range. The range is line of sight and will bounce around buildings. With base antennas on a house or building on each end, you can talk for 10 to 20 miles. Car to car could be up to two or three miles depending on the terrain between. It is legal to have a repeater (relay) station on GMRS but there are not many of them around. If you do have one in your area you can talk for 30 to 50 miles using a handheld radio. Mobile and base radios can be pricey.

MURS (Multi-use Radio Service)

MURS is a relatively new VHF service. It consists of five channels taken from the business radio service. Radios are limited to two watts transmitter power. VHF is a better choice than UHF in most instances. VHF travels farther on lower power. MURS handhelds have removable antennas like GMRS. This means you can use a car antenna or base antenna at home. This will give you about two miles car to car and 10 to 20 miles depending on height of antennas on both ends and the terrain between. There is a company called Dakota Alert that sells MURS radios and driveway and motion detector radios. They are weather proof and the batteries will work for months. You could set a few of these up at the perimeter of your property to alert you of intruders. These are one watt radios and will work over a long range. When an alarm is tripped it sends a recorded voice message on one of the five channels. You can have one of your radios tuned to the same channel as the alarm(s) and hear the alert.

MURS also allows data transmission. Hams created a system of data transmission that can also be used on MURS. This system is called Packet Radio. You can send messages similar to instant messaging and most Packet systems have a mailbox so messages can be stored and read later. This system is slower than dialup but is faster than I can type or read! Also, the Automatic Packet Reporting System (APRS) in use by hams that allows GPS location of stations or vehicles can legally be used on MURS.

There is almost zero activity on MURS (around Tulsa, anyway). I monitored all five channels for great lengths of time and the only thing I heard was Walmart on channel four. Since they use this mostly in-store there shouldn't be a problem with interference.

MURS radio is presented in depth in Chapter 4.

Summary of non-ham services:

Very short range

　　FRS/GMRS talkies

Moderate range

　　GMRS radios / repeaters

　　MURS

　　CB

Of all these Citizen's Radio Services, MURS is the most versatile and has capabilities of 2-meter VHF ham radio except for repeaters (relay stations).

Practicing vs. disaster operation

Remember, the word "PREpare" starts with "PRE" – before. With any preparedness activity you must practice ahead of time. Don't wait until a disaster is upon you and you have to dig out the manuals for your radios.

Practice regularly and be sure all your loved ones know how to operate the radios and know what your schedule is.

Schedules

Plan a schedule for contacting your loved ones. For practice you may set a certain time say, noon, or at the top of every even hour. In a real disaster you may want to try on the half-hours as well or even every 15 minutes. Write down the schedule and give everyone a copy.

Identity

Use first names only and do not ever give out exact locations. When a disaster strikes, the quiet MURS channels may suddenly come alive. Be polite but don't give yourself away. If you don't want to use names, assign tactical names. Charlie Seven and Alpha One won't give you away. Do the same with locations. Don't use "HQ" as your home base, how about Crooked Oak (assuming there is nothing named that in your area). You get the idea.

Legal note

The FCC rules state that you must not use secret codes or ciphers. However, you must decide if it is more important for the safety of your loved ones. In a real disaster nobody is going to be looking for someone using a little code language. One exception – on ham radio frequencies you should avoid code names, etc. Hams are very good at direction-finding and if you break the rules you may find yourself found and, if not turned in to the FCC, at least get ready for a good talking-to.

Scenarios

At the mall, lake or vehicle caravans no more than a mile apart: FRS talkies will work fine. In a car, be sure to hold the antenna vertically for the best range. Use a different channel if you hear other people on your channel. Use MURS talkies for better range and more privacy. CBs work well in caravans. You also can hear traffic reports from truckers.

In your neighborhood, FRS talkies will work fine unless you have big hills. MURS will work better but you may still have to stay near the tops of the hills for reliable communication.

Neighborhood with a central control operator at a house: If the control operator can stay upstairs, use FRS. MURS is better. An outside antenna can be used at the house. You can buy an outdoor MURS antenna online. Mount the antenna on the chimney or on a pole. Be aware of neighborhood covenants that forbid antennas. In this case, an antenna can be mounted in an attic.

Neighborhood with a control operator in a vehicle: Use MURS. Buy a magnetic mount MURS antenna and use it in the car. The car should be located at the highest point of the neighborhood, if possible.

Communicating with family in a car from your house: Use MURS with a magnetic mount antenna in the car and an outside antenna at the house. Range will vary based on the height of the antenna at the house. You should be able to talk a few miles unless the terrain is very hilly. CBs will work, also.

Communicating across town: Use MURS and an outside antenna at each house. Depending on height of the antennas and the terrain, you should be able to talk ten miles or more with this setup. You will get similar results with CBs but be aware of noise and interference factors.

For longer distances than these you will need ham radio.

CHAPTER 4
MURS RADIO IN DEPTH

My choice of a license-free radio service is MURS for reasons given throughout this chapter. MURS radios operate on VHF frequencies very close to amateur radio's 2-meter band. The 2-meter band is widely used for local communication, especially in emergencies. I think of MURS as a "junior" 2-meter band.

Dakota Alert has a series of MURS radios that will be used for the scenarios offered here. Here is the Dakota Alert handheld radio:

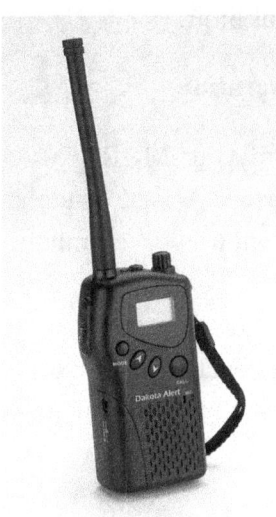

(Photo credits and website links are in the Resources chapter)

Here is a home base unit:

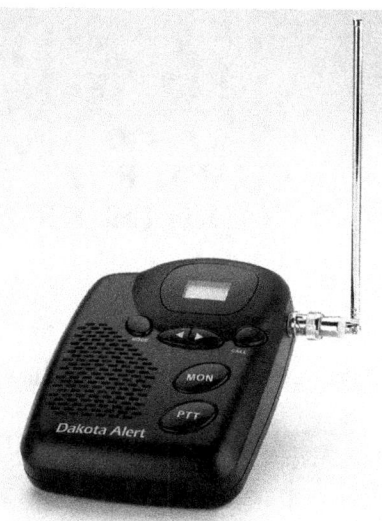

When the attached antenna is used on the base unit you will get about the same range as the handheld. These radios transmit with 2 watts of power, the legal limit.

House to handheld operation

To increase the range of your MURS system, an antenna external to the radio must be used. A base antenna can be mounted on a pole attached to your house or chimney or to a well-mounted antenna tripod and mast. A telescoping pole is helpful to easily hide a back yard antenna and extend it for use. If you live in a neighborhood with covenants that exclude any type of radio antennas, you can mount a base antenna in your attic.

Here is a base antenna:

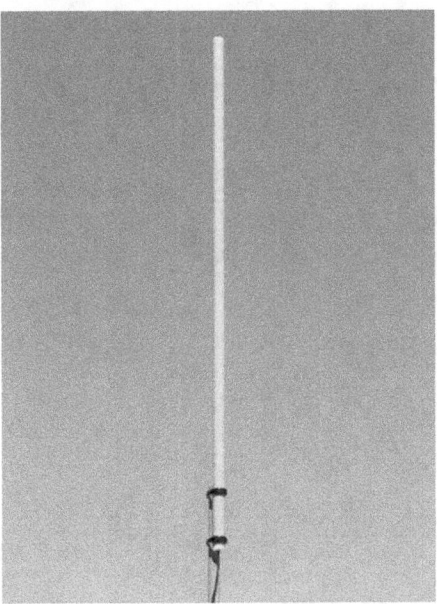

This antenna is slightly less than five feet tall. A base antenna can more than double your range when talking to someone using a handheld radio. Keep the antenna as close to vertical as possible for best range. Note: the base radio is not required. You can connect a base antenna to a handheld radio by first disconnecting the attached antenna and plugging in the base antenna cable. You may need an adapter to connect the cable properly. Let the antenna vendor know which radio you wish to connect to the antenna and they can advise you if an adapter is necessary.

Mobile operation

It is not advisable to use any of these radios inside a car unless you are in a closely spaced caravan. The metal in the car body degrades the signals. Magnetic mount antennas are available.

Here is one example:

The best place to attach a mobile antenna is in the center of the roof (watch out when entering your garage). If this is not possible, the trunk lid of a sedan or front fender of an SUV will suffice. Run the antenna cable through an open window. You can run the cable through the door but be aware that the cable could become crimped and short out the wires inside.

Mobile to mobile operating success depends on the terrain. On a highway or in level rural areas, you may be able to talk for several miles. In a city, with many buildings and other obstructions, you may not find you can talk as far but the range will still be much farther than handheld to handheld.

Mobile to base

With the mobile and base setups described above, a home station may be able to talk to a mobile station up to ten miles, depending on terrain and buildings in between.

Base to base

The best range for MURS radios is between base stations. Antennas should be as high as possible but not more than 20 feet above the highest part of your house or apartment. In a dire emergency, use the highest antenna possible. You be the judge if you need to exceed the 20 foot rule. Range from base to base could be as far as 25 miles if both antennas are as high as possible.

Neighborhood and city networks

The scenarios above are the best for your family and friends' communication. You can also use MURS for your neighborhood group or a larger city group. Use handhelds in your neighborhood with a base station as the control point of your neighborhood network. If you have an organized communication group with your church or city, several control points can be set up at base stations. These could be community centers, shelters, hospitals or homes in neighborhoods. Check for existing organizations already in place in your city that you can join. If none exist, create your own.

Motion Detectors

Dakota Alert also makes a motion detector radio that is weatherproof and runs for months on batteries. You can mount the motion detector radio on a fence post or an outside wall. Set the channel number on the detector to a channel other than the one you normally use to talk. Have a radio inside that is set to this channel. When something trips the motion detector, the radio will transmit a pre-recorded voice message saying that there is an alert in a certain zone. Up to four zones can be set up. Each zone has a different numbered alert message.

Here's the detector:

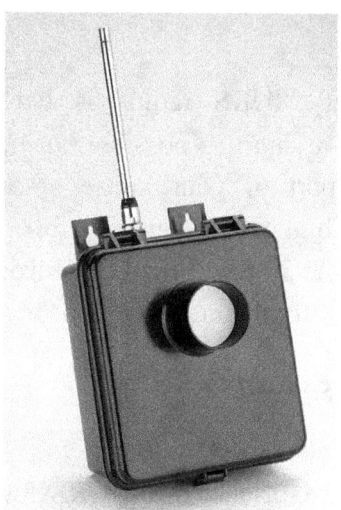

If you use a Dakota Alert base radio for receiving alerts, there is a relay connection on the base radio that can be used to connect a bell or siren alarm that is much louder than the voice alert messages.

Data

It is beyond the scope of this book, but MURS can also be used to transmit data. The hams' "packet radio" system is well-suited for MURS, though the data rate is slow. It is still fast enough for text messaging over radio. Also, the "Automatic Packet Reporting System" (APRS) that runs over packet radio can be used to track GPS locations of people and vehicles.

Summary

- The MURS citizen's radio service is similar to hams' 2-meter band.

- MURS allowed 2 watts transmit power is good for neighborhood and city coverage.

- External antennas extend the range of MURS radios.

- A base antenna can greatly extend range at a house, even in the attic.

- A mobile antenna is essential for operating in a vehicle.

- MURS gives much better range than FRS talkies.

- Neighborhood and city-wide networks can operate on MURS.

- If you need to talk more than about 25 miles, ham radio is the answer.

CHAPTER 5
INTRODUCTION TO HAM RADIO

What is amateur radio? Why is it called ham radio? The Amateur Radio Service is recognized as a valuable service of trained volunteers that serve as communicators in times of disaster as well as a hobby in normal times. The Amateur Service has its own section of rules, Part 97 of the United States radio rules. Here is the first statement in the rules:

The rules and regulations in this part are designed to provide an amateur radio service having a fundamental purpose as expressed in the following principles:

(a) Recognition and enhancement of the value of the amateur service to the public as a voluntary noncommercial communication service, particularly with respect to providing emergency communications.

(b) Continuation and extension of the amateur's proven ability to contribute to the advancement of the radio art.

(c) Encouragement and improvement of the amateur service through rules which provide for advancing skills in both the communication and technical phases of the art.

(d) Expansion of the existing reservoir within the amateur radio service of trained operators, technicians, and electronics experts.

(e) Continuation and extension of the amateur's unique ability to enhance international goodwill.

There is a tremendous responsibility for hams to abide by the rules. There are also many privileges for hams, such as high power and thousands of frequencies to use.

The word "Amateur" refers to not being paid for communicating, as opposed to paid radio operators. There is nothing "amateur" about ham radio. Most hams are well-trained and many build their own equipment and antennas.

The word 'ham" has many supposed origins but the one that is probably true is this: in the beginning of radio, ships and shore stations shared the airwaves with amateur experimenters. When there were a lot of amateurs on the air and interfering with commercial operators, the commercial ops would say, "Those hams are jamming you!" This is in the sense of movie star hams wanting all the attention.

Why the licensing requirement?

With privileges come responsibilities. A well-trained amateur knows when his radio is interfering with other services and how to fix the problem. Some ham frequencies allow transmissions to reach foreign countries. The U.S. has treaties with other countries pertaining to amateur communications between them. The amateur exams cover all aspects of radio communication within the U.S. and between the U.S. and other countries.

In the past the amateur exams have been very difficult, and the Morse Code test has eliminated many people from the amateur service even if they were competent in radio theory. There is no longer a Morse Code test requirement. There are three levels of amateur licenses. The Technician license, which is the entry-level license, gives privileges in all amateur VHF and UHF (local) bands, Morse Code in some international shortwave ham bands, and voice (SSB) in one shortwave band. The Technician exam is 35 questions. The General license exam is 50 tougher questions and gives many more privileges than the Technician license. The Amateur Extra license is the highest level and, hence, the toughest 50 question exam.

The Technician license has plenty of privileges for your preparedness communication needs. A few hours of study and taking online practice tests should be all you need to pass this test.

There are two other licenses that you may hear on the air. One is the Novice class. This was formerly the entry-level license. It is essentially equivalent to Technician now. The other is the Advanced class. Advanced privileges are higher than General but less than Amateur Extra. It was a stepping stone between the General and Extra but is no longer offered, and is noted here for historical information. Novices and Advanced operators can keep their licenses indefinitely.

How to determine if you want to get a ham license

Ham radio can help you in two major ways. You can be in touch with your loved ones for longer distances. Also, you can join a local group that conducts emergency nets in your area. This can keep you in touch with your neighborhood, city and state. If there is an emergency and your family is okay, you can volunteer to help with the community at large.

You may be hesitant to take this leap into the amateur radio service. You don't have to pass a test in order to listen. As a matter of fact, it is legal in the U.S. to listen to ANY frequency on the air with the exception of analog cell phone frequencies. A special law was enacted that forbids the reception of these cellular calls. That it was totally unenforceable was overlooked by the legislature. Today there are no analog cell transmissions. They are all digital.

So, you may buy ham equipment or scanners or handheld radios that work on amateur frequencies and listen all day long. This is all perfectly legal. *But to transmit you must pass the exam and obtain a license.* If listening is all you need, then don't worry about a license. Just don't transmit illegally. If, on the other hand, you would like to join a great hobby / service you can pass a reasonably simple exam to get your foot in the door.

Amateur Radio Emergency Groups

Look for amateur radio clubs in your area. You do not have to be licensed to join a club. The best information on what emergency services and repeaters are available in your area will be found there.

ARES / RACES

The Amateur Radio Emergency Service (ARES) and the Radio Amateur Civil Emergency Service (RACES) are usually the same group of hams. RACES was formerly a service that was put into effect by a state or the federal government during a declared emergency. ARES handles any emergency operation, government or otherwise. You must be licensed to participate in ARES / RACES. Each state has an ARES / RACES organization. Search online for your state's ARES / RACES website.

Skywarn

Skywarn is a group of radio operators that are trained in weather spotting, especially for tornados and severe storms. Skywarn hams report conditions and actual sightings of tornadoes directly to a ham at the National Weather Service. Find out what the Skywarn frequencies are in your area and listen to weather reports before the broadcast stations get them!

How and where to listen on VHF/UHF, Repeaters

The most-used band for local communication is the 2-meter VHF band. The 2-meter band frequencies are from 144 to 148 MHz. There are relay stations on 2-meters in many communities. These are called repeater stations. They allow hams to use handie-talkies to talk through repeaters for 30 to 50 miles or farther. Repeaters are located on tall buildings or TV and radio towers. Usually a repeater is sponsored by a radio club. Club members pay dues which are used to maintain the repeaters. The American Radio Relay League is a nation-wide association of amateur operators. They publish a Repeater Directory that contains the locations and frequencies of repeaters across the U.S. Repeaters can be heard on scanners, handheld receivers and, of course, ham handie-talkies.

Besides chit-chat, repeaters are used for Skywarn and ARES / RACES nets, emergencies of all kinds and coordination of parades, bike races, marathons, etc.

Hams also have a UHF band from 420 MHz to 450 MHz. There are repeaters on this band. They also are listed in the Repeater Directory.

How and where to listen on shortwave

Ham shortwave reception was briefly described earlier. Here are some more ham shortwave bands. Hams call these HF (high frequency) bands.

160 meters – 1.800 to 2.000 MHz LSB
75/80 meters – 3.500 to 4.000 MHz LSB
40 meters – 7.000 to 7.300 MHz LSB
20 meters – 14.000 to 14.350 MHz USB
17 meters – 18.068 to 18.168 MHz USB
15 meters – 21.000 to 21.450 MHz USB
12 meters – 24.890 to 24.990 MHz USB
10 meters – 28.000 to 29.700 MHz USB

160 through 20 meters are day and night bands. 17 meters through 10 meters are daytime bands. LSB is used below 20 meters and USB is used on 20 meters and higher frequencies. This is by convention rather than for any technical reason. Some of these bands will have Morse Code (CW) at the lower end of the band and voice operation (SSB) starts above that.

Ham lingo, Q-signals and Call Signs

Hams have many acronyms, abbreviations and other expressions they use when talking to one another. Here is a small sample of these so that you can follow along when listening. A male ham is referred to as "old man" or OM. Even a young boy is called an OM on the air. Females are called "young ladies" (YLs). An 80-year-old grandmother is still a YL! An OM's wife is referred to as his XYL (ex-young lady). If she is also a licensed ham, she is still a YL when she is on the air. An SWL (shortwave listener) is someone who is interested in radio but not a licensed ham.

Ham radio started out as Morse Code only. The technical term for Morse Code is CW (continuous wave). Hams took abbreviations from land telegraph operators and used them on CW. Some are abbreviations of English words, such as CU AGN (see you again). Roger (R) means received ok. There are number codes: 73 means good luck, 88 means hugs and kisses. A group of three-letter codes is used, called Q-codes because they start with the letter Q.

QTH = current location. QRM = interference from other stations. QRN = static. A link to the most-used Q-signals is in the Resources section.

When hams started using voice transmission they continued using Q-signals and other abbreviations, even when unnecessary. A ham may say "My QTH is Denver" instead of "I am located in Denver."

When communication is not clear, hams will repeat words and use a "phonetic alphabet" to spell words. "My name is Brad – Bravo Romeo Alpha Delta – Brad." The phonetic alphabet the hams use is in the Resources section.

A two-way communication between hams is called a contact, or a QSO. The act of making the contact is called "working" as in "I worked New Zealand the other day on 15 meters."

Every ham operator is assigned a unique "call sign" used to identify them. This call sign is assigned to hams in the U.S. by the Federal Communications Commission (FCC). Call signs consist of one or two letters followed by a single digit, followed by one, two or three letters. U.S. call signs start with A, N, K or W. Examples: W5BS, W1AW, KE5EHM, KL7ABC, AA5V, N5RFW, W0KIE, K5OVT. The number is one of ten assigned amateur regions in the U.S. The combination of the first letter(s) and the number is called the prefix. Prefixes in other countries use different letters.

Examples: XE1 = Mexico, VE5 = Canada, ZL3 = New Zealand.

Local contacts sound different from shortwave long distance contacts. Here's an example of a shortwave (HF) contact:

W5BS: CQ CQ CQ, CQ CQ CQ. This is W5BS, Whiskey Five Bravo Sierra, Whiskey Five Bravo Sierra, W5BS, calling CQ and standing by for a call.
(CQ means calling any station)
PY1TX: W5BS, W5BS, this is PY1TX, Papa Yankee One Tango X-ray, in Resende, Brazil. How do you copy, over?
W5BS: PY1TX, Papa Yankee One Tango X-ray, this is W5BS in Tulsa, Oklahoma – Tango Uniform Lima Sierra Alpha, in Oklahoma. My name is Brad - Bravo Romeo Alpha Delta - Brad. Your signal is 5, 9 - fifty-nine. Back to you. PY1TX, this is W5BS, go ahead.
(Shortwave contacts usually start with the exchange of names, locations, and signal reports and perhaps weather reports. The report "59" consists of readability, 1 = worst, 5 = best and signal strength, 1 = worst, 9 = best.)

When the conversation is finished, each station will announce the other station's call sign, his own call sign, and say "clear."

Contrast this with a local contact on a repeater:

WB5ABC: WB5ABC mobile, monitoring. (Listening and available for a call.)
W5BS: WB5ABC, W5BS, name is Brad.
WB5ABC: Hello, Brad, name here is John, passing through Tulsa. Home QTH is Dallas.
(conversation)
WB5ABC: Thanks for the shout, Brad. See you next time.
WB5ABC.

W5BS: OK, John, 73. W5BS

In a local contact a signal report is not usually given, as static-free FM is used. Also, the stations don't say "clear" when they are finished. It is implied in the conversation.

Both of these examples are normal contacts, not emergency communications. A formal directed net (network) operation will be evident in disasters.

Summary

- Amateur (ham) radio is a hobby / service licensed in the U.S. by the FCC.

- Hams have privileges beyond the license-free services due to passing an exam and adhering to high standards.

- It is legal for any person to listen to hams. To transmit and carry on two-way conversations on ham radio you must pass the exam and obtain a license and call sign.

- Amateur groups or clubs that carry on emergency communications are ARES, RACES. Skywarn and others.

- Local hams can be heard on 2-meters (VHF) and 420 MHz (UHF).

- Repeaters allow wide-area communication using handheld radios.

- Long distance communication is found on ham shortwave frequencies.

- Hams have their particular language of codes and abbreviations.

- Emergency ham communication is conducted with orderly, directed nets.

CHAPTER 6
HOW TO OBTAIN A HAM LICENSE

Whether you desire a ham license for emergency family communication or as a new hobby, you will be joining over 700,000 operators in the U.S. plus thousands more in other countries. Japan alone has over one million hams. There is no age limit requirement for a ham license in the U.S. Many children pass the Technician exam. You can, too.

Exams

As mentioned in Chapter 5, the entry-level ham license is the Technician license. This is a 35 question test covering elementary electronics theory, radio theory and rules and regulations. This test is somewhat technical but not difficult if you study the material. The test is administered by a group of hams called Volunteer Examiners (VEs).

How to study for the Technician exam

The VEs have developed a standard pool of questions for the Tech exam. The Tech question pool contains over 300 questions, all multiple-choice. Questions for the exams are randomly chosen by computer and printed for your session. Since you don't know which questions will be on the test, you must read through the entire question pool to get familiar with them. It is beyond the scope of this book to present these, but I can recommend two books that will help you study and pass and get your Technician license.

I teach a Technician study class, and the book that I use is "Technician Class 2010-2014" by Gordon West, Master Publishing, Inc. It is available on Amazon for $20.50. Another book is "The ARRL Ham Radio License Manual," available from The American Radio Relay League, arrl.org, for $29.95. These books list all the questions, with all the multiple choice answers. The wording of the questions and all answers remain the same for all tests. The order of the answers may change, so don't try to memorize answers by A, B, C or D. If a question is particularly difficult for you, you can memorize the correct answer by a keyword in that answer.

There are websites that have practice exams. Most of these are free of charge. Once you have studied the material and read through the questions, take the practice tests online. You can take them as many times as necessary. When you complete a test, the website will tell you which ones you missed and why. Keep taking the sample exams until you can consistently score 90% to 95% and you will have no problem passing the real test.

Electronics theory needed

Some knowledge of Direct Current (DC) circuits and a little of Alternating Current (AC) will be needed for the Tech exam. There are questions about batteries; instruments that measure voltage, current and resistance; and how to convert AC to DC and DC to AC. You will have to identify simple electronic components, such as resistors, capacitors, inductors and transistors.

Electronic circuits are represented on paper and in computer graphics by a set of pictures known as a schematic diagram. You will need to identify components in a circuit and now how to measure their values. A standard method of calculating values in a circuit is Ohm's Law. This simple set of two equations describes the relationships among voltage, current, resistance and power in a circuit. You will be allowed to bring a calculator to the test. The formulas are simple multiplication and division. Scientific notation is needed for values that vary widely – megahertz (MHz), picofarads and millivolts, for example.

Radio theory needed

Beyond elementary electronics, there are questions about Radio Frequencies (RF) and how radio waves are transmitted and received. An important topic is the relationship between frequency and wavelength. The range of radio communication can be determined by frequency, time of day and the effects of the sun on particles in the ionosphere. You will be asked to identify simple antennas and the proper cables to connect a transmitter to an antenna.

Rules and Regulations

Federal Communications Commission (FCC) Rules, Part 97, covers amateur radio. Hams must abide by the rules for many reasons. The U.S. must honor treaties with other countries since signals can go beyond our borders. Hams must know about safety around radio equipment and how make adjustments if problems arise, such as interference to other services. The complete rules are available on the FCC.gov website but you don't need to study all of them. Study the questions in the books.

Hams are identified by call signs, like W2XYZ or KH6ABC. These are assigned by the FCC. There are specific bands of frequencies assigned to ham radio and you must know the boundaries for Technician operators.

This may seem overwhelming at first, but the study books cover everything that will be needed for the test.

Find a VE testing session

How and where can you take the Technician exam? VEs give tests several times a month. Check with a local ham club for schedules. Check online with the ARRL VE site or W5YI VE site. These are the two major organizations that administer tests.

Summary

- To become a licensed radio amateur you must pass an exam.

- Morse Code is no longer a requirement for any ham radio test.

- Obtain a good Technician license manual.

- You must learn elementary electronics theory.

- You must learn rules and regulations pertaining to Amateur radio

- Volunteer Examiners administer tests in your area

CHAPTER 7
THE WOUXUN KG-UVD1P HANDHELD RADIO

Before you buy two-way handheld radios, please consider the information offered here about low-cost, dual-band, wide-coverage talkies.

There are handheld radios that have expanded coverage for transmitting as well as receive. Amateur radio handhelds are in this category. Hams call them "handie-talkies." Some talkies from the major ham manufacturers, such as ICOM, Kenwood, Yaesu and Alinco will transmit on VHF and / or UHF ham bands but have general coverage reception. If you will be using only ham frequencies for 2-way communication, then one of these will be your best choice. A dual-band 2-meter VHF and 440 MHz UHF talkie is a great choice for a beginning ham as it covers most local repeaters and net frequencies. Plus, you can listen to any frequency that is covered by the talkie's receiver.

The Wouxun KG-UVD1P handheld radio

There are other handhelds, especially many new ones from China that can be used as an all-purpose 2-way radio in more than one service. The Wouxun KG-UVD1P is a great example. It is a dual band VHF / UHF radio that works well on amateur frequencies but can transmit on other services' frequencies as well. This unit is FCC certified for use on MURS. However, you must set the transmit power to Low (1 watt) to be legal. The legal power limit for MURS is 2 watts but the high power settings on the Wouxun radio are 5 watts VHF and 4 watts UHF. Use discretion in an actual crisis as to whether you might want to use high power. If you are in a life and death situation nobody will care that you used a little extra power. This radio also covers GMRS and is legal if you have a GMRS license. As said before, the FCC is considering removing the license requirement for GMRS.

FRS channels can be programmed into this radio but two things make it illegal in the U.S. FRS is only allowed ½ watt power output. The 1 watt setting in this radio exceeds that. The other is that FRS must use a permanently attached antenna. This radio has a screw-in SMA connector which can be used for various external antennas. Again, discretion advised.

These Chinese talkies are perfectly legal on ham frequencies. They also receive weather broadcasts and FM broadcast radio. Prices are low compared to Japanese and US-made radios. The Wouxun KG-UVD1P will transmit and receive on all frequencies between 137 MHz and 174 MHz (VHF), and 420 and 520 MHz (UHF). This covers MURS, FRS, GMRS, business band and all ham 2-meter VHF and UHF frequencies.

Most of these radios can be programmed from a computer. You may have to pay extra for a data cable to connect to your computer. Transfer software is usually free. Small laminated reference cards are available online, so when programming in the field you don't need a computer or manual. Even though the computer programming is not required, it makes it easier to set up your channels and to copy the setup to other radios.

Programming the Wouxun handheld

"In the field" programming is covered in the Wouxun user manual and on a quick-reference card from "Nifty." This section assumes that you have a charged radio, programming cable and have installed the software that came with the cable or radio. There are two types of cables: serial and USB. Get the USB cable. The serial cable will only work with computers that have a serial port installed. The USB cable appears to the computer as a serial port (COM port).

Turn on the radio. Connect the data cable. It plugs into two jacks on the side of the radio. You will have to pry open a rubber cover to see the two jacks. The USB end of the cable, of course, plugs into your computer. Run the KG-UVD1P software.

Here's the opening screen:

On the menu, select Communication Port. A dialog box will pop up:

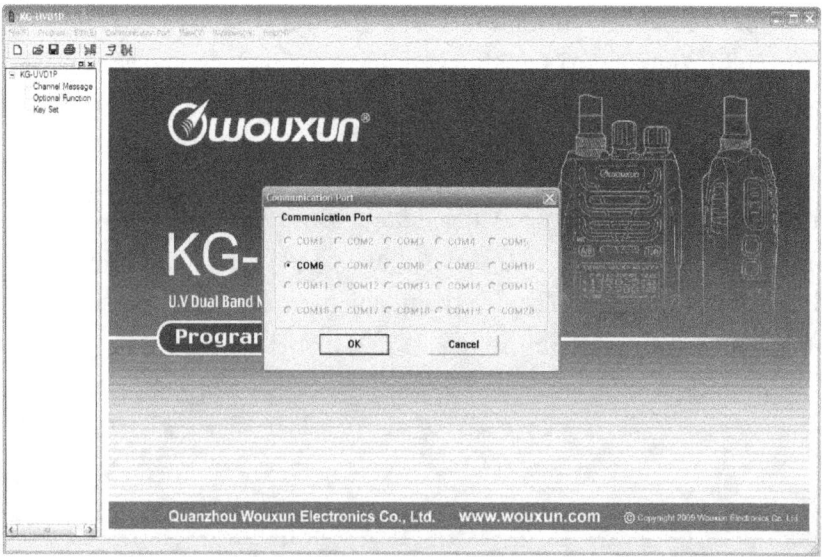

If there is more than one COM port available, you may have to try one, then another until you find the correct COM port. Click the COM port and then click OK. If this is the first time to program this particular radio, select File / New. A blank worksheet will appear:

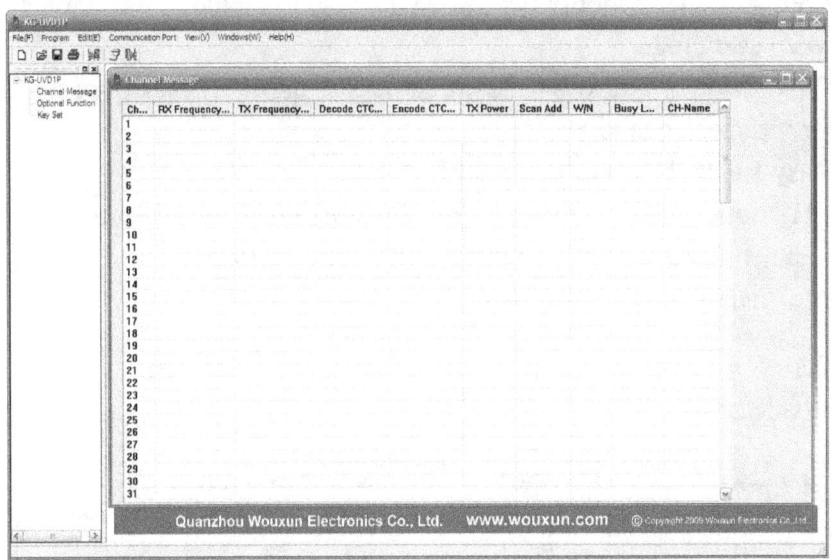

There are 128 memory channels. They do not have to be consecutive. You can enter a group of frequencies and leave blank channels before the next group. The blanks will not be selected when you switch between channels. The channel listing is filled out much like a spreadsheet. The columns are:

RX Frequency. This is the receive frequency in MHz for this channel. This is where you listen.

TX Frequency. Transmit frequency in MHz. This is the same as the RX Frequency for most channels. Repeaters will require a different TX frequency.

Decode CTC/DCS. This column has a drop-down list. Click the arrow to select the tone frequency. This is normally OFF.

Encode CTC/DSC. This is normally OFF but is used with ham repeaters.

TX Power. High power is 5 watts on VHF and 4 watts on UHF. Low power is one watt.

Scan Add. This should be ON if you wish to include this channel when scanning.

W/N. Wide or Narrow bandwidth. This is normally Narrow except for weather channels.

Busy Lock. This should be OFF.

CH-Name. Channel name. Up to 6 characters can be entered for a channel name that will be displayed on the radio display if you set it to "name" mode. (See below)

Here is a sample setup for MURS, FRS and a local weather broadcast station:

Ch...	RX Frequency...	TX Frequency...	Decode CTC...	Encode CTC...	TX Power	Scan Add	W/N	Busy Lock	CH-Name
1	151.82000	151.82000	OFF	OFF	High	ON	Narrow	OFF	MURS1
2	151.88000	151.88000	OFF	OFF	High	ON	Narrow	OFF	MURS2
3	151.94000	151.94000	OFF	OFF	High	ON	Narrow	OFF	MURS3
4	154.57000	154.57000	OFF	OFF	High	ON	Narrow	OFF	MURS4
5	154.60000	154.60000	OFF	OFF	High	ON	Narrow	OFF	MURS5
6	462.56250	462.56250	OFF	OFF	High	ON	Narrow	OFF	FRS1
7	462.58750	462.58750	OFF	OFF	High	ON	Narrow	OFF	FRS2
8	462.61250	462.61250	OFF	OFF	High	ON	Narrow	OFF	FRS3
9	462.63750	462.63750	OFF	OFF	High	ON	Narrow	OFF	FRS4
10	462.66250	462.66250	OFF	OFF	High	ON	Narrow	OFF	FRS5
11	462.68750	462.68750	OFF	OFF	High	ON	Narrow	OFF	FRS6
12	462.71250	462.71250	OFF	OFF	High	ON	Narrow	OFF	FRS7
13	467.56250	467.56250	OFF	OFF	High	ON	Narrow	OFF	FRS8
14	467.58750	467.58750	OFF	OFF	High	ON	Narrow	OFF	FRS9
15	467.61250	467.61250	OFF	OFF	High	ON	Narrow	OFF	FRS10
16	467.63750	467.63750	OFF	OFF	High	ON	Narrow	OFF	FRS11
17	467.66250	467.66250	OFF	OFF	High	ON	Narrow	OFF	FRS12
18	467.68750	467.68750	OFF	OFF	High	ON	Narrow	OFF	FRS13
19	467.71250	467.71250	OFF	OFF	High	ON	Narrow	OFF	FRS14
20	462.55000	462.55000	OFF	OFF	High	ON	Narrow	OFF	FRS15
21	462.57500	462.57500	OFF	OFF	High	ON	Narrow	OFF	FRS16
22	462.60000	462.60000	OFF	OFF	High	ON	Narrow	OFF	FRS17
23	462.62500	462.62500	OFF	OFF	High	ON	Narrow	OFF	FRS18
24	462.65000	462.65000	OFF	OFF	High	ON	Narrow	OFF	FRS19
25	462.67500	462.67500	OFF	OFF	High	ON	Narrow	OFF	FRS20
26	462.70000	462.70000	OFF	OFF	High	ON	Narrow	OFF	FRS21
27	462.72500	462.72500	OFF	OFF	High	ON	Narrow	OFF	FRS22
28	162.55000		OFF	OFF	High	ON	Wide	OFF	WX
29									
30									
31									

Notice that there is no TX Frequency for the weather (WX) station. You are not authorized to transmit on the weather frequency, so leave it blank. The weather channel TX Power will be ignored by the radio.

Save this into a file on the computer. Select File / Save and provide a folder and name for this file. Click Save.

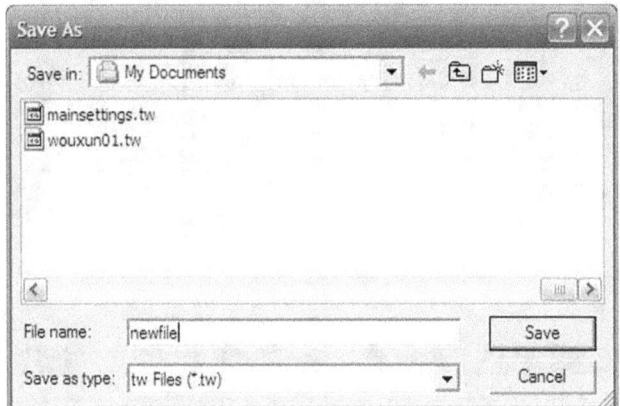

Next, write these settings into the radio. Select Program / Write to Radio. A progress bar will be shown as the data is written to the radio. If you receive an error message at this point, try another COM port. Now you can end this program and disconnect the radio from the computer.

The radio will now display the channels and frequencies you programmed. To set the radio to display the channel names, press the MENU button on the radio and use the up and down arrows to display menu number 21, CH-MDF. Press MENU again to move to the options line. Press up and down again until the display reads "NAME." Press MENU to exit. Now the names will display as you change channels.

Here is an example of a group of ham 2-meter frequencies:

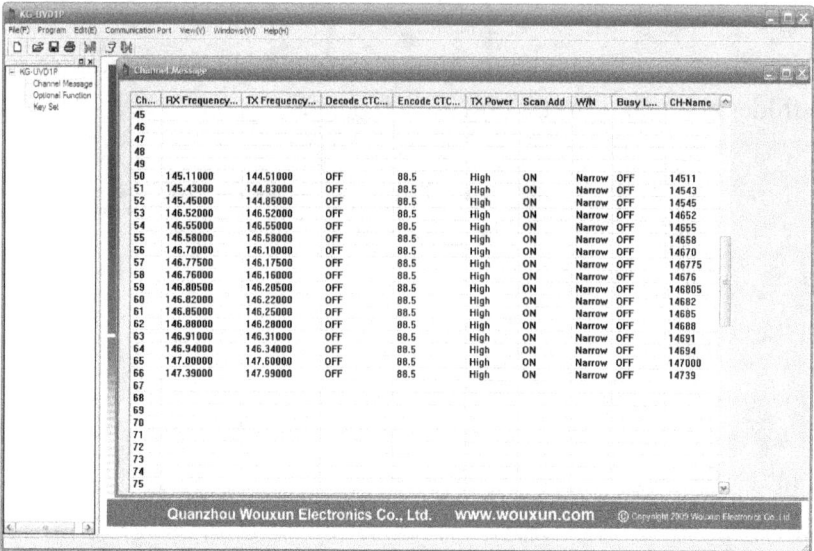

The channel names are just the frequencies. Some of these are "simplex" frequencies which means you transmit and receive on the same frequency. Repeaters have a different transmit frequency. For example, 146.88000 is the receive frequency for a repeater. The transmit frequency is 600 kHz below the receive frequency, or 146.28000. Repeaters in the 147 MHz range have a transmit frequency 600 kHz ABOVE the receive frequency. The repeaters also may have an Encode CTC/DCS. These will vary and the codes can be found through your local ham clubs or the ARRL Repeater Directory.

Cloning a radio

Cloning is copying the channel setup from one radio to another. Once you have your channel setup finalized (for now), you can use the same file to write to your other Wouxun KG-UVD1P radios.

If you want to clone from a radio that has a different setup than yours, first connect the radio to the computer as above and read from the radio:

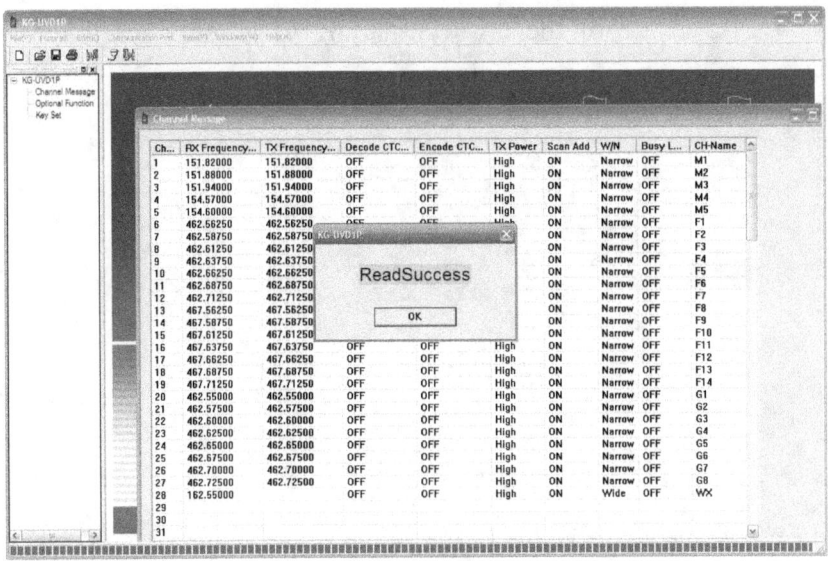

Now, save the file. Connect each radio to the computer and open this file from disk and write it to the radios.

Summary

- The Wouxun KG-UVD1P is a cost-effective, multi-service capable handheld radio.

- The easiest way to program the radio is by using a computer.

- You can manually program the radio via the front-panel buttons.

- Using the PC software it is easy to clone or duplicate the channel setup to many radios.

- Plan your frequency list well, then enter the data on the spreadsheet screen.

- Be aware of the laws pertaining to all services that you program into this radio.

CHAPTER 8
A COMMUNITY LOW-POWER FM RADIO
STATION

Several years ago the FCC decided to open up FM station licensing for community, low-powered radio stations. The plan was to allow for 100 watt and 10 watt stations. This service is known as LPFM – Low-power Frequency Modulation. Originally, even large cities would have had allocations for lots of stations. But the National Association of Broadcasters and others lobbied the FCC to tighten up the spacing restrictions from established high-power stations so much that large cities had no allocations and smaller towns may have had only one or two.

Consequently, some individuals or groups who had applied for LPFM licenses were left out in the cold and decided to build their stations without becoming licensed. These are generally known as "micro FM" stations due to being small stations running very low power. Some people call them "pirate" stations. No, they are not legal in the US. Some of these stations have been shut down by the FCC and assessed fines of $10,000 or more.

Why would a community need a micro FM station?

Having said that, why would a small community want to take a chance? The stations that are caught and fined are the ones that transmit 24/7 and are blatantly defying the rules, or the ones that are turned in by someone. In a truly wide-spread and long-term disaster, a micro FM station may be the only way to get news to a community. Many people will not have ham radios or FRS or MURS radios. But they will almost all have an FM radio.

What information would be aired?

The micro FM station in a disaster would broadcast news and perhaps weather. Where would this information come from? The owner of the micro FM station or a supporter should be a ham radio operator or at least be able to listen to ham frequencies. You can be sure that even in the worst disasters, there will be ham networks on the air. News can be heard on Amateur Radio Emergency Service (ARES) nets. Your state has an ARES net. There are national ARES nets. News can be gathered from these and also from individual hams in various places.

If no weather service is available, hams may come through. Lots of hams have small weather stations. Some of these actually transmit weather information through a 2-meter packet (digital) system called Automatic Packet Reporting System (APRS). APRS is known chiefly for GPS locations of ham stations. Weather is also reported through APRS. Some of these weather stations report to a computer and have some simple forecasting software.

Schedules

Here is one scenario for micro FM. The ham operator or listener gathers information from ham nets and weather stations during the evening hours or in the morning. The first broadcast is scheduled for noon. The micro FM station operator can turn on the transmitter at noon and read the information live over the air. The report may also be recorded and then played back at this time. The report can be scheduled for re-broadcast at, say, 2:00 PM and 6:00 PM. If there is new news or changes, they can be noted on these later broadcasts. No music should be played except as a station ID or to attract attention from the community. Note: transmissions are short and to the point. This is no time to play DJ. It is unlikely that this station will be shut down and fined by the FCC – especially when the information may save lives or property.

Equipment needed

A micro FM system requires a source of audio, such as a microphone or a computer; an antenna and antenna cable; a tower or other support for the antenna; and a transmitter. We will discuss these starting with the antenna and working backwards.

Antenna, support, and cable

There are two types of antennas to be considered for micro FM. One is an omnidirectional vertical antenna. This antenna is better for a station that is located inside the community. Coverage will be approximately in a circle around the station location. The other antenna is a vertical "beam" antenna. This is better for a station that is off to one side of the community and is pointed in the direction of the center of the community.

An example of an omnidirectional antenna is the Comet CFM-95SL.

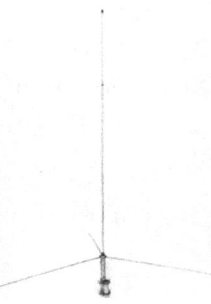

This antenna has some gain, which means that the power that reaches the antenna will be effectively multiplied. For example, if 10 watts of power reaches the antenna, it may be effectively doubled to 20 watts effective radiated power (ERP). This antenna can be ordered online for about $100.00 plus shipping. This antenna should be tuned to your frequency of choice. An instrument called an "antenna analyzer" or "SWR analyzer" will help tune the antenna. You adjust the antenna by lengthening or shortening it at a joint between two aluminum tubes. A ham operator will know where to borrow or buy an antenna analyzer.

An example of a vertical beam is the Comet CD-95Y.

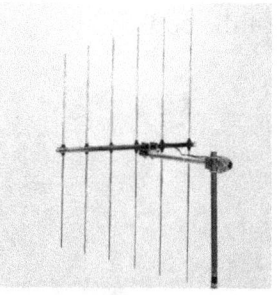

This antenna has more gain than the omni. Your ERP will be multiplied by 4 or more. Your 10 watts will transmit with 40 watts or more ERP. This antenna is very expensive, about $300.00. Antennas can also be home-built for low cost. There are instructions for building them in the *ARRL Amateur Radio Handbook* or the *ARRL Antenna Book*, both available from arrl.org.

Either of these antennas can be supported by a pipe, telescoping mast, or a chimney or vent pipe mount. Height is your friend. The higher the better, but the support should be stable. If a tower is available the antenna can be mounted at the top or from the side at any height using a stand-off mount.

The cable that connects the transmitter to the antenna must be selected carefully. A great type of coax cable is Belden 9913. This is very stiff but the signal will suffer low losses from the cable. Try to limit the run of cable to 100 feet or less if possible. The longer the cable, the more signal is lost. These antennas have a characteristic called "gain" which means the effective radiated power (ERP) in watts from the antenna will be more than the power in watts supplied by the transmitter. This helps to overcome coax cable losses.

Transmitter

Transmitters can be found online. Ordering can be tricky. Some companies will make you fill out a sworn statement that you are going to export this radio outside the U.S. Buying from another country seems risky but they don't require any statement of intent. The resource section has links to websites that sell transmitters. The price range is wide – a few hundred to a few thousand dollars. Power levels vary with price. A 10 or 15 watt transmitter should be fine for a community station. If you have hilly terrain you may want to locate the antenna as high as possible and perhaps use 25 watts.

Select a transmitter that operates on 12 volts DC. If household electrical power is available, a power supply that converts 120 volt house current to 12 volts DC can be used. A car battery or marine battery can be used if AC is not available. If you run the transmitter from a car battery that is installed in a car, turn the car off while transmitting. This will ensure that no noise from the car's electronics goes out over the air.

Microphone or computer audio

If you want to do all your broadcasts live, all you need is a microphone. If a computer is available, you can use a program like Windows Sound Recorder or Audacity (free) to record the broadcasts. Connect the audio output from the computer's sound card to the line input on the transmitter. To play back the news or other sound clips you can use Windows Media Player or Winamp (free). You can make a playlist with either of these programs. If you want to repeat the playlist there is a repeat function in the software. Just stop when you have played it enough times for everyone to hear.

Testing

Once you get all the equipment set up and tested at the transmitter site, send someone out in a car to drive around the area and note how reception is in various parts of the community. If there are areas where reception is not good, try raising the power a bit or moving the antenna to a higher point. If you find that you are broadcasting well outside the community, turn the transmitter power down a bit.

Summary

- In an extreme, long-term disaster, a micro FM station can be used to keep the community informed.

- Keep transmissions short and to the point to not attract attention outside your community.

- Get installation help from a ham operator or other experienced radio personnel.

- Audio can be supplied by a microphone and /or a computer.

- Antennas are available online or you can build your own.

- Use low-loss coax cable from the transmitter to the antenna.

- Tune the antenna (if adjustable) using an antenna analyzer.

- Get the news from ham stations or distant broadcast or shortwave stations and re-broadcast to your community.

APPENDIX
RESOURCES

If any of the links are broken, just search for the item.

Chapter 1.

Photos: the author, Eton Corp., Uniden.

Emergency radios:
Eton Radios: http://www.etoncorp.com/GeneralMenu
C. Crane: http://www.ccrane.com/radios/

SAME county codes:
http://www.nws.noaa.gov/nwr/indexnw.htm#sametable
Uniden HomePatrol Scanner: http://www.homepatrol.com/
Icom handhelds:
http://www.icomamerica.com/en/products/receivers/handheld/r20/
default.aspx
AOR handhelds: http://www.aorusa.com/receivers/

Find a ham operator:
http://wireless2.fcc.gov/UlsApp/UlsSearch/searchAmateur.jsp

Chapter 2.

Shortwave station frequency info:
Popular Communications Magazine: http://popular-communications.com/
Monitoring Times Magazine: http://www.monitoringtimes.com/

Ham radio info
American Radio Relay League: http://www.arrl.org/
CQ Amateur Radio Magazine: http://www.cq-amateur-radio.com/

Chapter 3.

FRS: http://www.fcc.gov/encyclopedia/family-radio-service-frs
GMRS: http://www.fcc.gov/encyclopedia/general-mobile-radio-service-gmrs
MURS: http://www.fcc.gov/encyclopedia/multi-use-radio-service-murs-0
CB: http://www.fcc.gov/encyclopedia/citizens-band-cb-service

Chapter 4.

Photos:
Intercoms Online: http://www.intercomsonline.com/
Murs Radio: http://shop.murs-radio.com
DPD Productions: http://www.dpdproductions.com

Dakota Alert MURS handheld at murs-radio.com:
http://shop.murs-radio.com/MURS-Hand-Held-M538-HT.htm;jsessionid=5815A11D33F5DCFD08B6A92BE5268B00.q scstrfrnt04

Dakota Alert MURS base radio:
http://shop.murs-radio.com/MURS-Base-M538-
BS.htm;jsessionid=5815A11D33F5DCFD08B6A92BE5268B00.qs
cstrfrnt04

Puxing VHF handheld. Works on MURS and ham VHF (2-
meters):
http://shop.murs-radio.com/Puxing-PX-777-PLUS-VHF-Hand-
Held-Radio-
PX777PLUS.htm;jsessionid=5815A11D33F5DCFD08B6A92BE5
268B00.qscstrfrnt04

Dakota Alert Motion Detector / Transmitter: http://shop.murs-
radio.com/MURS-Alert-Transmitter-MAT.htm

TYT Dual Band Chinese Handheld – similar to the ones I have
(Wouxun):
http://shop.murs-radio.com/TYT-TH-UVF1A-Dual-Band-VHF-
UHF-Hand-Held-Transceiver-TH-UVF1A.htm

Wouxun Dual Band Chinese Handheld (the one described in
Chapter 7):
http://www.radioshop888.com/radioshop_product.php?id=103959

The Radioshop888 website is confusing and they sell many
handhelds of different brands. There are variations even within a
model number. I had no problem ordering and receiving products
from them even though they are in Hong Kong. I used PayPal for
payment just in case.

A car antenna for MURS only:
http://www.firestik.com/Catalog/MURS45.htm

Some home and car MURS antennas:
http://www.dpdproductions.com/page_murs.html

Chapter 5.

Amateur Radio FCC Rules & Regs: http://www.arrl.org/part-97-amateur-radio
Amateur Radio Emergency Service: http://www.arrl.org/ares
Skywarn: http://skywarn.org/
Amateur Frequencies: http://www.arrl.org/frequency-allocations
Q-codes:
http://en.wikipedia.org/wiki/Q_code#Q_codes_applicable_for_use_in_amateur_radio

Chapter 6.

Books:
Technician Class 2010-1014: http://www.amazon.com/Technician-Class-2010-2014-Gordon-West/dp/0945053622
ARRL License Manual: http://www.arrl.org/ham-radio-license-manual

Exams:
ARRL Volunteer Examiner Exams: http://www.arrl.org/find-an-amateur-radio-license-exam-session
W5YI VEC Group: http://www.w5yi.org/

Online Practice Exams:
AA9PW: http://aa9pw.com/radio/
QRZ.com: http://www.qrz.com/ht/
eHam.net: http://www.eham.net/exams/

Chapter 7.

Photos:
Wouxun website: http://www.wouxun.com/
Computer screen grabs Wouxun Software

Wouxun Dual Band Chinese Handheld:
http://www.radioshop888.com/radioshop_product.php?id=103959

Laminated reference cards:
http://www.niftyaccessories.com/Wouxun_RefGuides.htm

Chapter 8.

Photos: The Antenna Farm website:
http://www.theantennafarm.com/catalog/index.php?main_page=index&cPath=191_193_258_976_944

FCC LPFM Licensing: http://www.fcc.gov/encyclopedia/low-power-fm-broadcast-radio-stations-lpfm
Transmitters:
Progressive Concepts: http://www.progressive-concepts.com/
PCS Electronics: http://pcs-electronics.com/

Antennas:
http://www.theantennafarm.com/catalog/index.php?main_page=index&cPath=191_193_258_976_944

Coaxial cable:
Cable X-perts, Inc.: http://www.cablexperts.com/cfdocs/index.cfm
The Wireman: http://www.thewireman.com/coax.html

ABOUT THE AUTHOR

Brad Smith has been a licensed amateur radio operator for over 40 years. He has communicated via CW, AM, SSB, FM, Amateur Television, Packet Radio and other modes over the years. Brad's day job is slaving over a hot computer all day as a Software Engineer. His family tolerates his tech toys.

www.ingramcontent.com/pod-product-compliance
Lightning Source LLC
Chambersburg PA
CBHW072339290526
45794CB00002B/944